Hooked on Meaning

Barry Lane

Discover
Writing
Press
www.discoverwriting.com

Hooked on Meaning

Writing Craft Video Lessons
that Improve Achievement
on Writing Tests through
Authentic Instruction

For Students Grades 3-8
Teacher Study Guide

Barry Lane

Discover
Writing
Press
www.discoverwriting.com

Discover Writing Press

P. O. Box 264
Shoreham, VT 05770
800-613-8055
www.discoverwriting.com

ISBN 10: 1-931492-19-0
ISBN 13: 978-1-931492-19-5

06 07 08 09 10 11 12   10 9 8 7 6 5 4 3 2

Printed in Canada

To the teachers and children of the future.
May you get the schools
you deserve,

not the trials
you don't need.

Table of Contents

Appendices

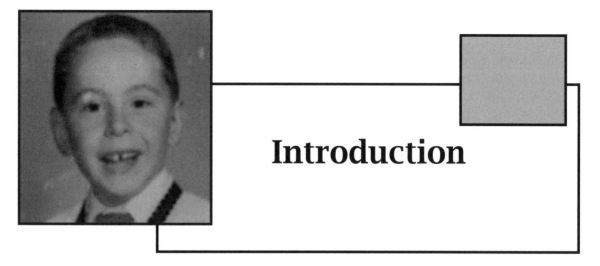

Introduction

To assess how you really feel about the purpose of writing tests, take a moment to do this simple test.

What is the Purpose of Writing Tests?

a) To assess progress of student writers and improve performance of schools.

b) To improve the bottom line of testing and textbook companies and help politicians get re-elected.

c) To assist real estate agents in selling more houses.

d) To teach students how to master simple writing formulas.

e) All of the above.

Turn the page for the answer.

If you answered **a**, you are idealistic and naïve.

If you answered **b**, you are political and a bit cynical.

If you answered **c**, you just bought a house.

If you answered **d**, you are practical but misguided.

If you answered **e,** you answered correctly!

And, unfortunately, you feel confused and powerless. You think you can't teach the way you want to because some test-score-crazed bureaucrat is peering over your shoulder. You end up doing things that do not really support children in becoming better writers simply because your school district is telling you to do it or because it will enhance the test score data. You didn't become a teacher to help data. You became a teacher to help students.

In the back of your mind, you suspect all these tests will not really help children become better writers. You don't like thinking this way because it makes you feel alienated from your colleagues and distant from administrators, who speak at length about improving school performance, rubrics and standards.

You try to believe in tests, for the sake of the kids, so you buy a workbook on how to construct proper paragraphs. You hang posters of hamburger essays and inverted pyramids in your classroom. All your students know what topic sentences are and you watch as the twinkle slowly dissolves in their eyes and transforms into an audible groan whenever writing time comes around.

You complain to colleagues that children do not like writing anymore and that, before all the testing, you were a better, more creative teacher of writing. You did writing workshops ALL the time. You had a 3rd grader who wrote a novel in your class. Now your students do not write novels, they write sentences and paragraphs. They write supporting details.

You decide you need to escape this mass hysteria and put the test in its place. Writing should be a joyous activity—hard work, but joyous. You want your students to be hooked on meaning again, and you know in your heart that these inspired writers will have no problem scoring the highest on the writing test.

I Created *Hooked on Meaning* for You

The *Hooked on Meaning* DVD and teacher guide is both an antidote to the toxic effects of testing and a tool for improving test scores. From my experience as a teacher and writer, I know that the kids do best at writing when they are relaxed in mind and knowledgeable about all the craft choices at their disposal. Formula writing promotes a singular way of teaching writing, and it produces singular results. When a student is hooked on meaning, they care about what matters and, as a result, their individual voices rise to the surface. They are able to make a writing prompt personal and craft their ideas into unique structures.

This is why a writer's workshop is the best way to teach writing. Students who write regularly on topics of choice, who know how to craft their OWN idea into an interesting story, can turn even the blandest of test prompts into something extraordinary, something personal. On the contrary, students who are always told what to write about create essays in the robotic spirit of those who simply do what they are told.

But if you haven't started a writing workshop yet, don't despair. You can still use this video to give your students permission to write outside the box and improve their attitudes and results on writing tests. For help with beginning a writing workshop, I have also included a list of resources in the annotated bibliography.

How to Use This Guide and Video

This guide and video program is meant to be a shot in the arm for you and your class near test time. The twelve short sections and accompanying activities explore ideas such as finding out our attitudes towards writing tests, crafting language, adding dialogue, injecting meaningful elaboration, interpreting your own truth and shaping essay responses in unique, personal ways. Watch the lesson with your class and do the accompanying exercise. Use the teacher study guide and support materials to create more mini-lessons near the week of the test.

A Word About the Order of the Lessons

Most writing instruction goes from lessons in idea development to lessons on grammar, word choice, etc. This video goes in the opposite direction, starting with lessons on strong verbs, sentence structure and transitions and moving toward big picture issues such as text structures, sensory detail and using imagination. The reason I chose this jumpy organization was to encourage teachers to use this video non-sequentially, jumping from pithy lessons on verbs to more big picture lessons like creating new text structures.

After you have looked through the video yourself, I suggest you review both the main and supplementary lessons in this guide and decide where to begin with your students. For a quick reference you can also look at the diagnostic chapter guide on the inside front cover of the book. Here you can decide on lessons based on problem areas in student writing.

This Teacher's Guide gives step-by-step directions for each lesson, suggests supplementary lessons and gives you posters and reproducible forms to support these lessons in your classroom. I have tried to make it as clear-cut as possible and supply you with all the material you need to teach these mini-lessons. More lessons and student examples will be posted in the teacher center at www.discoverwriting.com. This guide is designed to supplement the short video segments that you can show directly to your class.

As you see in the video, wherever possible, I have tried to add humor to lighten the mood and create interest. I believe that humor can be a great doorway into the heart of a learner. It's also one of the rare things in school that hasn't been state-mandated yet. I believe there needs to be more fun in school—for the sake of both teachers and students—especially at a time when panic about test scores reigns supreme. When we laugh, we acknowledge a shared truth. This unites us in a common understanding. Getting hooked on meaning doesn't always have to be a serious endeavor.

However you may choose to use these lessons, it is my greatest hope that you will find they relieve some of the burdens of testing and turn some of life's lemons into lemonade. It's hot out there. Drink with me!

Barry Lane

Who Reads Writing Tests?

The Point

When students take a writing test, they have very little sense of their audience. They are writing to a wall. No wonder their writing often sounds as flat as a Nebraskan ski slope. Students are empowered to take control of their audience when they can imagine who is reading their work. Show this first chapter the week before the test to give students a sense of audience and lighten up the attitude about testing. Post some of their pictures around the classroom.

Try This 1: Who is Your Audience?

Talk to your students about who will read their writing test. What do they look like? What could their job be like? Have students try this:

1. Draw a picture of your reader before they read your writing test.
2. Draw a picture of your reader after they have read your piece.
3. Share your pictures with your classmates. How do they look different?
4. Create a Portrait Gallery of test scorers in your class. (See the Gallery of Test Scorers chapter on the DVD and a sample overhead on the next page.)
5. Use the poster on page 8 to give students concrete strategies for preparing for the test.

Discussion

What is the test scorer looking for on the writing test? How is writing for the test different from "real" writing?

What's at the End of the Rainbow?

Writing tests can be oppressive to both teachers and students. That's why it's always inspiring when students use their imagination to express their true feelings about testing while taking the test. The idea in the following piece of writing was created by an anonymous 4th grade student from Connecticut and relayed to me by his teacher. Use it as an example of how a student can express any idea on a writing test, even ideas that speak against the test itself.

When I crawled to the top of the rainbow, I could feel the sun beating down hard on my face. I had shimmied my way up the slippery colors, and I had finally made it. But not for long, because I felt myself sliding down the other side, the side everyone always talked about, the side they wrote songs about. I slid faster and faster. The wind blasted through my hair, and I could feel my whole body sliding through the clouds and soon my feet touched the ground.

I couldn't believe it. I was standing there, on the front lawn of my grandmother's farmhouse and there was Molly, my Grandma's dog, alive again. A moment later I was sitting in my grandmother's kitchen. My grandma, who I haven't seen in three years since she died, was there. I sat there sipping Grandma's fresh lemonade from the mason jar. Grandma didn't believe in using real glasses. It was in that moment I realized I must be in heaven. Yes, this was heaven.

That's when I noticed a door I'd never seen before. I asked Grandma where it went and she told me not to pay any attention to it. But when she left the room, I opened it.

It lead down a dark stairway into a dark cellar I had never seen before. I walked around a corner and saw a long hallway. Suddenly, I felt myself falling through space. I landed in a dark cavern, like an old barn or warehouse. Pigeons fluttered up in the rafters and shafts of light streamed in from holes in the roof.

At the end of the warehouse was a doorway framed in light. I could feel myself being drawn to it, like a moth to a flame. As I reached for the doorknob, I realized I wasn't in heaven anymore. I was in the other place. And what did I see . . . ?

Kids, sitting at desks, doing writing prompts.

How to Prepare for a Writing Test

Relax

Read the prompt

Re-Read the prompt and **underline** key parts

Plan what you want to write

Write a few leads

Start with a Spark

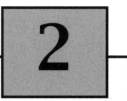

Make Verbs Strong Engines

The Point

Verbs are the engines of sentences and the key to any language. A weak verb is like a weak engine and will not propel a story forward with any strength. As students learn to use strong verbs, their writing will take on more texture and voice.

What You Do

Watch the video chapter on re-verbing. Talk about the verb as being the engine of the sentence. Read sentences with weak verbs and do the following "Re-Verbing" exercises. Have students practice re-verbing their own writing. Find a piece of writing with strong verbs and copy it on an overhead. Ask students to identify the verbs as you circle them on a transparency.

Try This 2: Re-Verbing

You can soup up the engine of any story by re-verbing. Read the following sample sentences and replace the weak verbs with stronger ones. How does the writing sound different now?

The boy <u>went</u> outside.

In this sentence, the reader has no idea why the boy goes outside. Let's try using a stronger verb.

The boy <u>tiptoed</u> outside.

Now the reader knows there is someone else in the house and that the boy does not want them to know he is going outside. Verbs propel a story and add flavor and meaning.

Discussion

Why do stronger verbs improve writing? Is there a time when weaker verbs are better?

Soup up the verbs in these sentences.

1. The sinister man <u>went</u> into the bank lobby.

2. The scared child <u>went</u> into the haunted house.

3. The clumsy ballet dancer <u>moved</u> across the stage.

4. "SIT DOWN!" <u>said</u> the angry man.

Strong Verbs Propel Writing

Listen to the verbs in the following piece of writing. They are the words printed in bold. Compare the verbs in this writing with the verbs in the same piece on the next page. Notice how exact, specific verbs improve writing. Strive to make verbs specific in your own work.

When I **arrived** in Cairo that spring night, my body **filled** with new perceptions of an exotic world. At the airport, people **pushed** close together and **flowed** as one river down the long corridors. The men in long robes **made** strange **hissing** noises as though **whispering** to each other in some language only they knew. On the streets, Policemen **waved** their Kalishnikov rifles at little cars that **plowed** through red traffic lights. Donkey carts **limped** along with dusty buses and tiny insect-like cars that **flitted** around, horns **beeping** constantly like angry bees.

Strong Verbs Propel Writing - Part 2

When I **came** to Cairo that spring night, my body **experienced** new perceptions of an exotic world. At the airport, people **pushed** close together and **went** as one river down the long corridors. The men in long robes **made** strange noises as though **talking** to each other in some language only they knew. On the streets, Policemen **held** their Kalishnikov rifles at little cars that **drove** through red traffic lights. Donkey carts **moved** along with dusty buses and tiny insect-like cars that **drove** around, horns **sounding** constantly like angry bees.

Create Unique Sentences

3

The Point

To do well on a writing test, students need to know how to write in complete sentences. When they know the parts of a sentence, it is easier to understand the different kinds of sentences. With this knowledge, they can manipulate their thoughts in unique and creative ways. In writing workshops, where students write on a regular basis on topics of choice, understanding the grammar of sentences can be a ticket to freedom.

What You Do

If you want to have some fun, try speaking to your students without using complete sentences. String together a few phrases like this: "Hello. Working on making sentences. Fun to do. Lunch good today. Waiting for homework. Wonder why need sentences. Any ideas?"

When students start scratching their heads, talk about why sentences are important and the parts of a sentence. Explain how all sentences are constructed with a subject, a verb and a predicate. Have students label sample sentences, such as:

Subject   **Predicate**
The dog   *put the slipper in the toilet.*

Try This 3: Ba Da Bing Sentences
From *Reviving the Essay: How to Teach Structure Without Formula* by Gretchen Bernabei

Teacher Gretchen Bernabei has a great way to move students from short, declarative sentences to compound, complex sentences. She teaches her students to write *Ba Da Bing Sentences*—a sentence that describes where you are, what you saw and what you thought. Here are the steps to creating a Ba Da Bing Sentence. You can also find them on the video. Have your students try this:

1. Draw a picture of a foot, an eye and a thought bubble.
2. Think of an event to write about.
3. Ask yourself where your feet went, what you saw and what you thought. Make it into one sentence.

4. *Example:* As I walked into the kitchen and saw my mother sitting at the table, the clock chimed 2 AM and I thought, "This doesn't look good."

Discussion

Can Ba Da Bing sentences improve your writing? Are there times when it is better not to write in complete sentences?

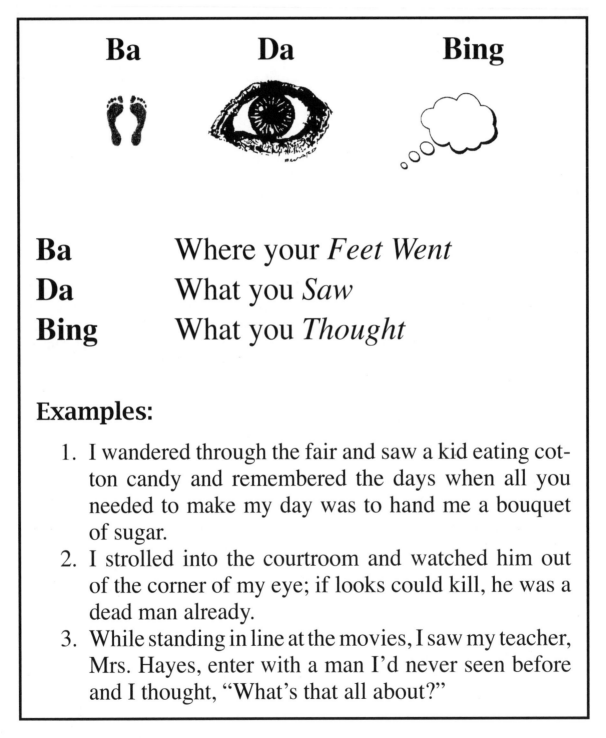

Ba   Where your *Feet Went*

Da   What you *Saw*

Bing   What you *Thought*

Examples:

1. I wandered through the fair and saw a kid eating cotton candy and remembered the days when all you needed to make my day was to hand me a bouquet of sugar.
2. I strolled into the courtroom and watched him out of the corner of my eye; if looks could kill, he was a dead man already.
3. While standing in line at the movies, I saw my teacher, Mrs. Hayes, enter with a man I'd never seen before and I thought, "What's that all about?"

Try This 4: Varying Sentences

Writing can sound monotonous if the sentences are all made the same way. Read these two pieces. Notice how in the first piece the sentences all begin the same way and in the second piece the sentences vary. In your test response writing, try varying your sentences. For ideas on how to vary sentences, see "A Field Guide to Sentences" on page 14.

Example 1

I think my grandma is a special person. I really liked it when she taught me how to sew. I liked it when she taught me to make apple pies. I liked it when she taught me to play Uno. I like it when she lets me stay up late on Saturday nights. I like it when we look up at the stars.

Example 2

My Grandma is a very special person. She has taught me to sew, bake apple pies and how to play Uno. On Saturday nights, we stay up late and just sit on the porch and look up at the stars.

Take a piece of your own writing. Circle the first word of every sentence. If you notice many begin with the same word, try rewriting the sentences for a better flow.

A Field Guide to Sentences

The Basic Sentence

I love writing tests.

The Compound Sentence

I love writing tests and I also love liver.

The Complex Sentence

Although I like cold spinach and liver, writing tests can be fun, too.

The Compound-Complex Sentence

Apart from my love for you, I love writing tests and liver the most.

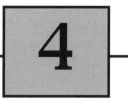

Create New Text Structures

The Point

Traditionally, students are taught to write essays in the form of a hamburger paragraph:

Top bun: *Topic Sentence*
Meat: *3 Supporting Details*
Bottom bun: *Conclusion*

Well-meaning teachers want to show students a basic structure to model their writing after, which, even when done well, tends to make students' essays sound exactly the same and a bit phony. In the past, writing scorers rewarded this type of formula writing with the highest scores, but not anymore. Today's readers are looking for qualities like voice, vivid detail, fluency of thought and idea development. Stilted writing might get a passing score, but will never rate the highest.

The most prized writing has a varied structure that tracks a student's own thoughts and perceptions. For this type of writing to occur, students need permission to experiment with many different structures.

Show the video chapter on varying sentence structures. Then, experiment with some of the structures on the following pages. These include the fable/moral structure depicted in the video and many others described on the following pages. For detailed lessons and more examples, see Gretchen Bernabei's book *Reviving the Essay: How to Teach Structure Without Formula.*

What You Do

Show your students a traditional hamburger paragraph. Then show them some alternative text structures that appear in the "Hamburger Helper" section.

Experiment putting the same information into different paragraph structures. Paragraph structures lead to text structures. Try writing the same information into two of the text structures.

After showing students many examples, ask them to experiment answering a test prompt using two different text structures.

Chapter 4

Discussion

How can paragraphs vary from one another? What happens to the voice in writing when all paragraphs are the same? What makes a great paragraph?

Hamburger Helper

There is more than one way to grow a paragraph. In this lesson, we practice playing around with different hamburger paragraphs. Here are three. Make them into paragraphs on a separate page and then try making your own unique burger. See examples next page.

The Classic Hamburger

- Topic Sentence
- Supporting Detail
- Supporting Detail
- Supporting Detail
- Concluding Sentence

The Topical Whopper

- Topic Sentence
- Topic Sentence
- Topic Sentence
- Question

The Fake Out Burger

- Fact or statistic
- Fact or statistic
- Fact or statistic
- Question or statement that negates or questions the facts

The _____ Burger
(You make it up)

A Field Guide to Burgers

The Classic Burger

No surprise here, but you can tell your students to use this format if they want to make sure they include all their best arguments in a logical way. Tell them this is only ONE way to organize an essay.

There are three reasons why I believe school uniforms are important. The first reason is they make people of all economic backgrounds more equal. The second reason is that uniforms will help eliminate social cliques that revolve around how you dress. The final reason I think school uniforms are important is that they create less distraction for students who want to learn and not have to worry about how much of their naval is showing. In this essay, I will show you why these three reasons are enough for all schools to go to school uniforms.

The Topical Whopper

Here you get to spill all your ideas in the first paragraph, then maybe prove them one at a time in succeeding paragraphs.

School uniforms make people of all economic backgrounds more equal. School uniforms eliminate social cliques that revolved on how you dress. School Uniforms will remove unnecessary distractions and help everyone to learn more. Why have 10 years of public school led me to these conclusions?

The Fake Out Burger

Here's where the writer includes facts that support one opinion, then turns it around and explains why the facts are wrong.

Studies show schools that require school uniforms create an atmosphere of less social inequality. In a recent study, students found that social cliques disappeared once they were required to wear uniforms to school. Teachers have fewer distractions when they focus on teaching and not what their students are wearing. Students, too, concentrate on real learning.

These facts seem to support school uniforms. Let me tell you why they are wrong.

Create a Text Structure

Try This 5: Sequel to a Fable

Narrative writing is often shunned when older students are asked to write expository responses. Yet, stories are sometimes the best way to make a point. A Greek slave named Aesop proved that thousands of years ago in his famous fables. Aesop used storytelling as a tool to make a point. (We have included the pictures here or you can download color ones at www.discoverwriting.com.)

1. Read "The Tortoise and the Hare Continued." Stop after each extension fable and ask the students what they think the new moral should be.
2. After you have practiced for a while, give students a real fable, like the one in this chapter. Ask them to extend it and come up with a new moral.
3. As a class, share and celebrate the new morals.
4. Ask students to try writing a persuasive essay using this structure. Show students other structures from *Reviving the Essay* on the following pages.

Discussion

How does a fable/moral structure make a point differently than a more straightforward essay structure? How can you use this structure in your writing?

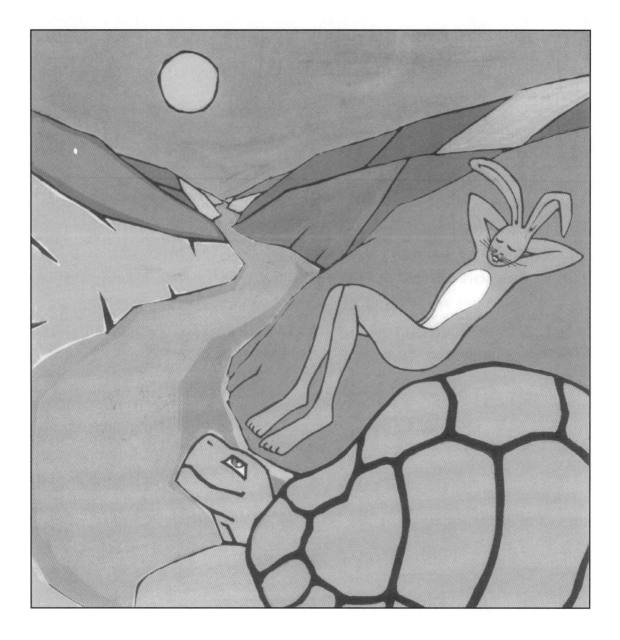

Slow and Steady Wins the Race

The Tortoise becomes a running star.

Hares challenge the Tortoise to another race and he agrees.

New moral: Quit while you're ahead.

Read the following fable. What happened the next day? What is the new moral?

The Ant and the Grasshopper

In a field one summer's day a grasshopper was hopping about, chirping and singing to its heart's content. An ant passed by bearing along, with great toil, an ear of corn he was taking to the nest.

"Why not come and chat with me," said the grasshopper, "instead of toiling and moiling in that way?"

"I am helping to lay up food for the winter," said the ant, "and recommend you to do the same."

"Why bother about winter?" said the grasshopper. "We have got plenty of food at present."

But the ant went on its way and continued its toil. When the winter came, the grasshopper had no food and found itself dying of hunger, while it saw the ants distributing corn and grain every day from the stores they had collected in the summer. Then the Grasshopper knew:

**It is best to prepare for the
days of necessity.**

Gretchen Bernabei's
Gallery of Text Structures

In her book, *Reviving the Essay: How to Teach Structure Without Formula,* and in her CD, *Lightning in a Bottle*, Gretchen Bernabei instructs teachers in how to experiment with a variety of text structures. Study the text structures on the following pages and try one or two with your class.

For detailed examples at all grade levels visit www.trailofbreadcrumbs.org

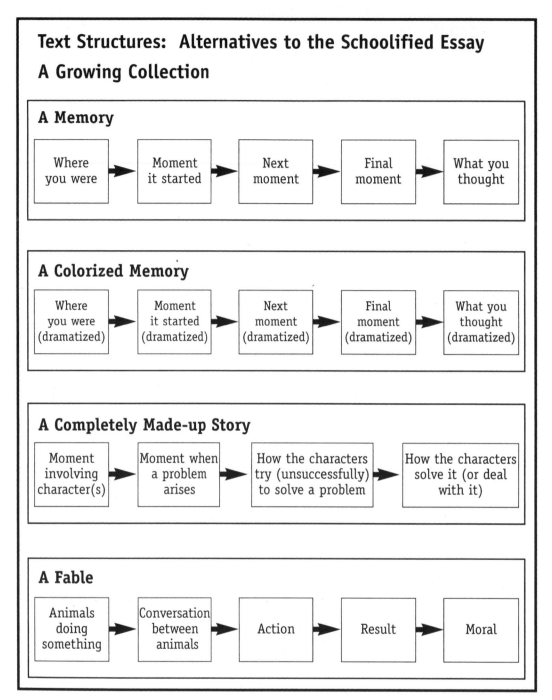

Text Structures: Alternatives to the Schoolified Essay
A Growing Collection

A Memory

| Where you were | → | Moment it started | → | Next moment | → | Final moment | → | What you thought |

A Colorized Memory

| Where you were (dramatized) | → | Moment it started (dramatized) | → | Next moment (dramatized) | → | Final moment (dramatized) | → | What you thought (dramatized) |

A Completely Made-up Story

| Moment involving character(s) | → | Moment when a problem arises | → | How the characters try (unsuccessfully) to solve a problem | → | How the characters solve it (or deal with it) |

A Fable

| Animals doing something | → | Conversation between animals | → | Action | → | Result | → | Moral |

For classroom duplication only. Enlarge at 121% for 81/2 x 11 sheet

From *Reviving the Essay: How to Teach Structure without Formula*, Gretchen Bernabei

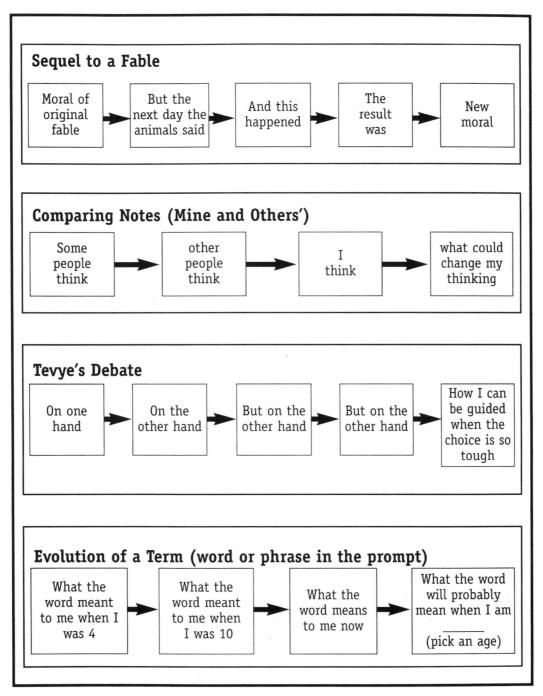

Sequel to a Fable

| Moral of original fable | → | But the next day the animals said | → | And this happened | → | The result was | → | New moral |

Comparing Notes (Mine and Others')

| Some people think | → | other people think | → | I think | → | what could change my thinking |

Tevye's Debate

| On one hand | → | On the other hand | → | But on the other hand | → | But on the other hand | → | How I can be guided when the choice is so tough |

Evolution of a Term (word or phrase in the prompt)

| What the word meant to me when I was 4 | → | What the word meant to me when I was 10 | → | What the word means to me now | → | What the word will probably mean when I am _____ (pick an age) |

For classroom duplication only. Enlarge at 121% for 81/2 x 11 sheet

From *Reviving the Essay: How to Teach Structure without Formula*, Gretchen Bernabei

Spin of a Coin: Finding the Paradox

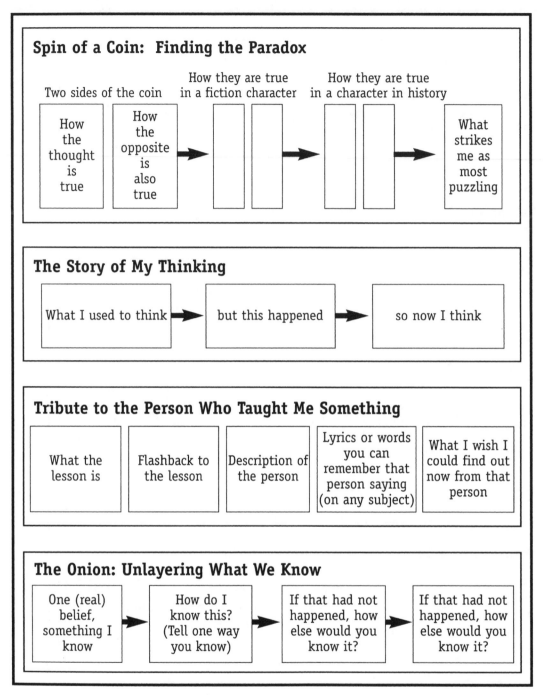

Two sides of the coin | How they are true in a fiction character | How they are true in a character in history

| How the thought is true | How the opposite is also true | | | | | What strikes me as most puzzling |

The Story of My Thinking

What I used to think → but this happened → so now I think

Tribute to the Person Who Taught Me Something

What the lesson is | Flashback to the lesson | Description of the person | Lyrics or words you can remember that person saying (on any subject) | What I wish I could find out now from that person

The Onion: Unlayering What We Know

One (real) belief, something I know → How do I know this? (Tell one way you know) → If that had not happened, how else would you know it? → If that had not happened, how else would you know it?

For classroom duplication only. Enlarge at 121% for 81/2 x 11 sheet

From *Reviving the Essay: How to Teach Structure without Formula*, Gretchen Bernabei

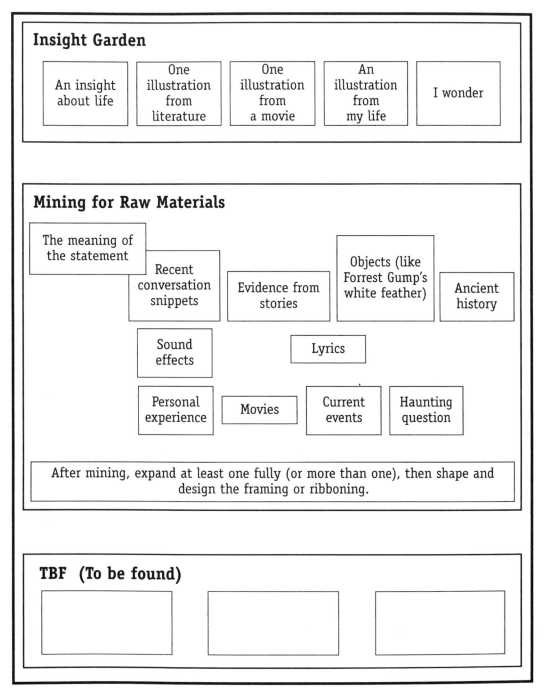

Insight Garden

| An insight about life | One illustration from literature | One illustration from a movie | An illustration from my life | I wonder |

Mining for Raw Materials

The meaning of the statement

Recent conversation snippets

Evidence from stories

Objects (like Forrest Gump's white feather)

Ancient history

Sound effects

Lyrics

Personal experience

Movies

Current events

Haunting question

After mining, expand at least one fully (or more than one), then shape and design the framing or ribboning.

TBF (To be found)

For classroom duplication only. Enlarge at 121% for 81/2 x 11 sheet

From *Reviving the Essay: How to Teach Structure without Formula*, Gretchen Bernabei

Steps for Writing a Good Essay

STEP 0: UNDERSTAND THE WRITING PROMPT.
Tips: Use the dictionary for any words you have questions about.
Look at the prompt from all angles.

STEP 1: FIND YOUR TRUISM.
Tips: Don't choose the first one that comes to mind.
Don't use it if you really don't think it's true.

STEP 2: FIND YOUR STRUCTURE.
Tips: You might need to invent your own.
You can change the order at any time.
Write one sentence for each part, to see if it hangs together.

STEP 3: PLAN OUT YOUR TEXT SUPPORT.
Tips: Your support can be not only from literature, but from your life.
Ask yourself questions like   "How do I know this?"
"Who in the literature does this?"
"Exactly when?"

STEP 4: DRAFT IT.
Tips: Pretend you're explaining it to someone and write what you'd say.
Pretend that other person is doubtful and you have to make it clear.

STEP 5: DESIGN YOUR FRAME.
Tips: Play with dialogue, lyrics, familiar words, quotations, story pieces, echoed phrases.

STEP 6: TRY IT ON A READER'S EARS.
Tips: Imagine that they can't see it, they can just hear it.
Try to get a reaction. Watch for: Huh? Okay! Ahhhh... Wow!!!!

STEP 7: MAKE IT READY FOR A READER'S EYES.
Tips: Use the dictionary for iffy spellings.
Check your citations and forms.

For classroom duplication only. Enlarge at 121% for 81/2 x 11 sheet

From *Reviving the Essay: How to Teach Structure without Formula*, Gretchen Bernabei

Paste in Transitions

The Point

What is the reader looking for who scores a student's writing test? Beyond having good ideas and a strong voice, they are looking for unity and connections between thoughts, ideas and paragraphs. A paper strong in ideas and voice but weak in transitions will often score lower than a paper with solid transitions. Beyond testing, transitions can help writers find their own sense of unity and connection with a piece. Transitions provide continuity throughout the writing that enhances the reader's ability to follow the writer's ideas and thought processes.

What You Do

Show your students a piece of string. Then slide beads on the string until you have created a necklace. Talk about how each bead on the string is like a paragraph and how the string is the thing that holds the paragraphs together. Without the string you would not have a necklace; you would have a handful of beads. In writing, it is transitions that create the string that holds the paragraphs together. Look on the next page for transition words and come up with some of your own. Play Transition Ball. See video or next page.

Discussion

Why are transitions important? Can you make transitions without transition words? How?

Chapter 5

Try This 6: Transition Ball

From *Learning on Their Feet: A Sourcebook for Kinesthetic Learning, K-8* and *Carol out of the Box* by Carol Glynn. Used with permission.

Here is a fun way to practice transitions without paper or pencil but with the whole class on the playground or sitting in a circle on the rug in your room. All you need is a beach ball and a class ready to have some fun.

Step One: Explain to students what transitions are and what they do in writing. How do transitions connect with ideas and paragraphs? Give examples of transitions like the ones mentioned on the video: moreover, consequently, later that day, etc. Ask your students why transitions are important. Find examples from literature to share; present on the overhead projector.

Step Two: Get a ball (a beach ball works well). Sit on the floor or stand in a circle with your class. Start telling a story and pass the ball to someone in the circle. They must continue the story, beginning with a transition.

Step Three: Encourage your students to get creative and lurch the story in an entirely new direction.

Rule: Because "then" is an overused transition and tends to weaken writing, *you can't use it*.

Transitions connect and move the story forward:

- Later that day
- A year later
- Twenty years later after he came back from Brazil

Transitions connect ideas together:

- Moreover
- Consequently
- Another way that

Use the
Five Senses

6

The Point

Using sensory detail is a great way to make a connection with your reader. The point is not to use all five senses whenever you write anything. Rather, the point is to be aware of the sensory options at your disposal as a writer. This mini-lesson is a reminder for your students to use their five senses.

What You Do

After you've done the lesson on the video (next page) hang the posters on the following pages in your classroom to remind students to use their five senses. Read literature with strong sensory details to your students. Fill the walls of your classroom with posters and pictures full of color, texture and light. Take students on walks where they record sensory detail in their notebooks. Ask students to bring their notebooks to a few ordinary places outside of school: a McDonalds, a supermarket, a library, a store. Ask them to sit for 10 minutes and record their observations. After they have written a page or two, ask them to read over their observations and circle those that are surprising.

Discussion

What does sensory detail do for writing? What senses do you use most in your writing? What senses could you use more often?

Try This 7: A "Come With Me" Poem

Think of a place to take the reader and write a "Come with Me" poem that transports the reader to this place. Each line of the poem begins with a new sense.

Come with me to _____

See

Hear

Feel

Smell

Taste

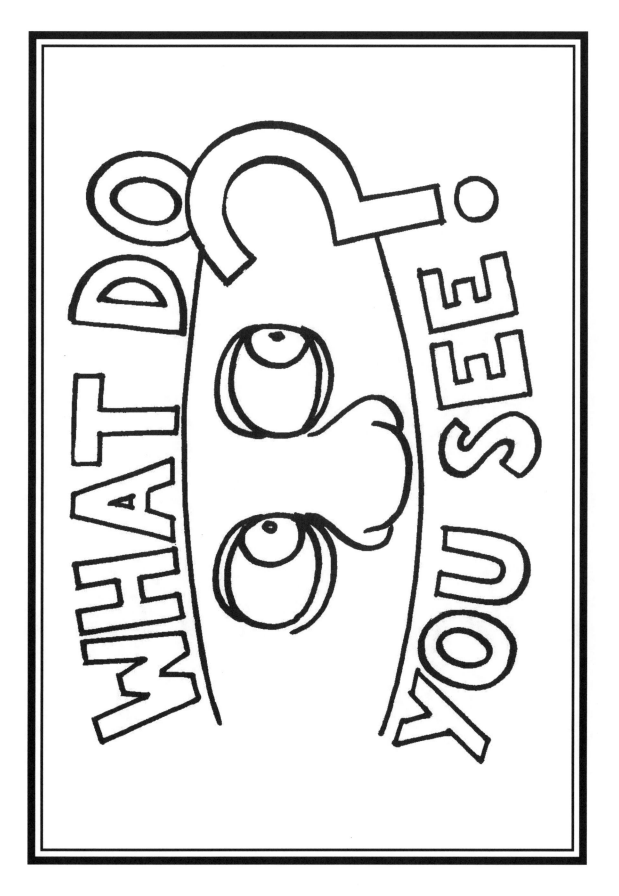

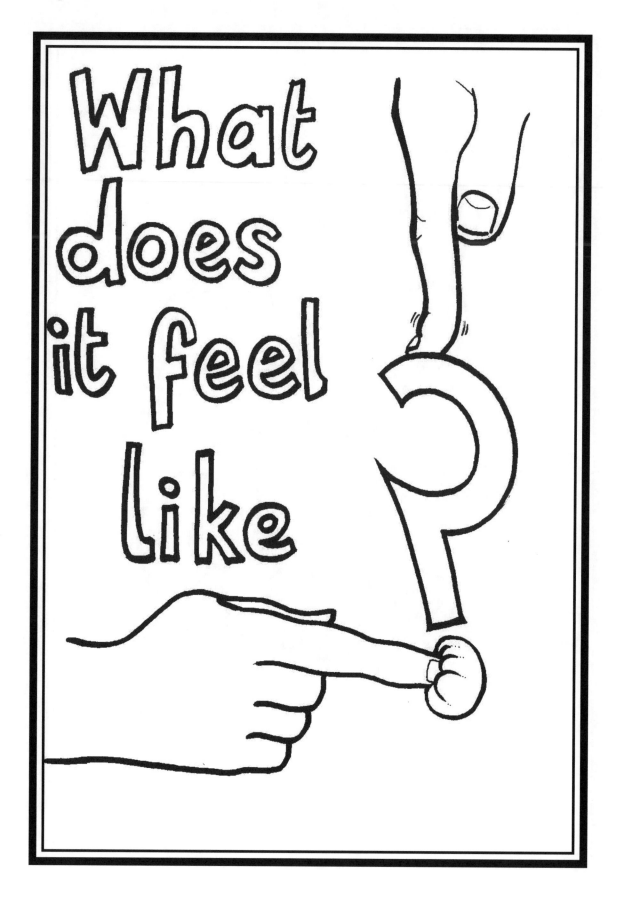

Build Bridges to the Reader's Mind

The Point

The main reason students perform poorly on writing tests is that they respond to a general prompt in a general way. For example, let's say the prompt is, "Write about a special person in your life." The standard response might sound like this:

My mother is a special person in my life. She takes me everywhere in her van. She's always taking me to gymnastics practice.

That may sound okay, but it's not very interesting. That response is not memorable and does not really make the reader want to keep reading. Now, let's get closer to something personal and specific right from the start and listen to the difference.

My mom's rolling down the highway at 70 mph, the steering wheel in one hand and my vocabulary words in the other.
"Intrinsic," she says in her soft voice and I search my brain for a definition as I munch on the Doritos and watch as she passes the tractor-trailer truck. That's my mom, taking me to my gymnastics lesson, always putting my needs before her own, always feeding me with guidance and love."

How do we teach students to personalize their response to an impersonal prompt? How do we help students to find their own truth instead of parroting the truth of the test?

The next six lessons on the video teach this in different ways. This lesson teaches students to have faith in their ability to interpret their own truth.

The next lesson encourages students to add real dialogue to bring personal voices into our writing.

Lesson 9, The Doubting Chorus, trains students to hear their own personal doubting voices in their heads and respond to those voices rather than a formulaic template, i.e. The five paragraph theme, etc.

Lesson 10 teaches students to start with a spark and add word pictures or snapshots throughout their writing. Student can use snapshots to help explode key moments in a narrative and make a test prompt their own.

Lesson 11 shows how to turn a prompt into a big moment to write about in slow motion.

The final lesson encourages students to use their imagination to generate interest in a test prompt.

What You Do

Begin by showing students photos with interpretive truths under them. See the following pages or use *Lightning in a Bottle,* a CD-ROM with 266 thematic images. Show the picture with its accompanying truism. Then have the students come up with their own truisms for their own pictures. Celebrate their multifarious interpretations. See excerpt from *Reviving the Essay* by Gretchen Bernabei. Then, have students try the activity.

Discussion

Do writing tests want you to write bland responses to the bland questions they ask? How do you take a boring question and give it an interesting answer? Does your truth matter?

Try This 8: Re-Writing a Prompt

We've all received a bland prompt on a writing test. The key is to try to come up with your own unique spin on that tired, old prompt. Here's one way to get creative with your writing prompt.

1. Take a prompt like "life has all kinds of adventure" and draw a picture to go with it. Remind your students that an adventure does not have to be a big exciting trip or a sky dive. An adventure for a kindergartener might be a first bike ride without training wheels.
2. Next, have your students write their own truth about the picture.
3. Finally, free write about the personal truth and drawing.

Point out to students how they started with a general prompt and how they have made it personal and unique. This is the path to success on most writing tests.

Behind the darkest clouds lies the sun waiting to break through.

Reprinted with permission from *Lightning in a Bottle*,
a CD-ROM with 266 pictures and thematic insights.
From *Reviving the Essay: How to Teach Structure without Formula* by Gretchen Bernabei.

Celebrate Truisms

Following are some examples of 4th graders' writings about the photo of the lock on the previous page. Notice all the unique interpretations they had about this one photo.

The future is locked until its moment. —Wesley

Everyone has a secret. —Brandon

Even something so small can make a big difference. —Sallie

Small things can hold everything together. —Lindsey

If you do drugs, you'll get locked-up. —Donald

There's always a key in life. —Jessica

Everyone gets in trouble. —Brandy

Some things can't be opened. —Victor

Not everything is unlocked for you. —Joel

Unlock your freedom. —Derek

You have to work to find the key to life. —Hillary

Some things are best sealed up. —Etan

From *Reviving the Essay* by Gretchen Bernabei

Don't write about a bird;
write about a robin.

Don't write about humanity;
write about your cousin Frank.

Don't write about Winter;
write about how your nostrils
freeze up on cold mornings.

Make it Specific.

Try This 9: Making a General Prompt Personal

To do well on a writing test, you must know how to take a general prompt and make it personal. Here is a quick lesson to help you learn this. Read the prompt and, in the box beneath it, write a personal memory that goes with the prompt and could serve as your response.

Write about a special person in your life.

Write about an exciting moment in your life.

What do Readers Want?

Personal Stories

Personal Connections

Text-to-Text Connections

Rich Detail

Snappy Leads

Try This 10: Make Text-to-Text and Text-to-Life Connections

Many writing tests reward students who know how to make text-to-text and text-to-life connections. The ability to make these connections also gives students creative ideas to add to their writings that will wake up their readers. Here is a mini-lesson that teaches students to make these connections and grow insights about their writing prompt.

1. Ask students to look at a photograph.
2. Have them write for five minutes about what the photo means to them.
3. Ask them to stop and read over what they have written.
4. Now, have them write for ten more minutes about a book, movie or play that this photo reminds them of and why.
5. Stop, take a breath and have them read over their writing again.
6. Now, have them write for another ten minutes about an experience that the photo reminds them of and why.
7. Stop and share the writing with a partner and with the whole class. Tell your students that their connections are what test scorers are looking for on the test.
8. Now try this same activity with a writing prompt.

This activity appears in a different form in the book, *Why We Must Run with Scissors* by Barry Lane and Gretchen Bernabei

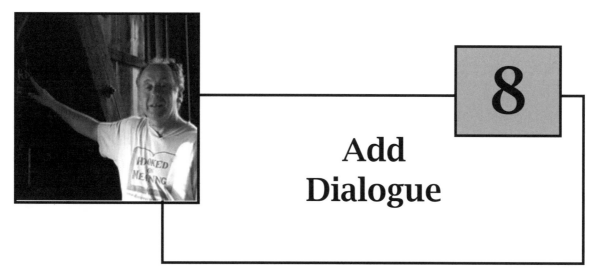

Add Dialogue

8

The Point

Dialogue brings an essay into the present and is one of the quickest ways to inject voice into a piece of writing. Most student writers have trouble using dialogue in small doses. You know the kind of writing I'm talking about—the kind where the dialogue starts but never stops. This lesson is about writing dialogue. I want students to see that they can use dialogue in small doses to pull a reader in at any time or place in a piece of writing.

What You Do

Talk to your students about what dialogue does in a piece of writing. Read an essay that uses dialogue in an effective way and then re-write it without the dialogue. What does it now lack?

Transform sentences that could be done as dialogue into dialogue. Encourage students to "think dialogue" at dramatic moments in their essays and work with them to develop a taste for dialogue by finding good bits of conversation in movies, TV and real life and sharing them with the class.

On the following page is an activity to help students practice writing effective dialogue.

Discussion

How does dialogue improve a piece of writing? When does it weaken it?

Chapter 8

Try This 11: Writing Great Dialogue Leads

Below are three prompts. Choose one and write a dialogue lead.

1. Write about an exciting time in your life.
2. Write about a special person in your life.
3. Write about a favorite toy.
4. Write about a special box in the attic of your house and the day you opened it.
5. Write about your position on school uniforms.

Example:

Write about a favorite toy.

"I will destroy you," he says in the deep garbled voice. He stands on my bureau in his long black robe. "No one can deny the power of the dark side."

I'm not sure if Darth Vader is my favorite toy, but it's the one I remember best.

Don't say the old lady screamed . . . Bring her on and let her scream

—Mark Twain

Chapter 1

Use dialogue when . . .

1. Things are dramatic.
2. You want to reveal a character.
3. You want to show, not tell.
4. You want to dramatize an idea.

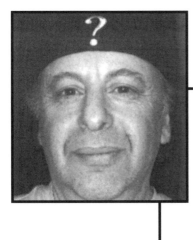

Listen to the
Doubting Chorus

The Point

Students who are taught to list three details after a topic sentence miss opportunities to respond to a real audience and their own internal sense of audience. The Doubting Chorus lesson from the video has been very successful in helping at-risk students pass persuasive writing tests with high scores. The reason for its success lies in its ability to translate the tricks of spoken language into written language. When students hear a real doubting voice in their own head, they have a cue to elaborate in a meaningful way.

What You Do

After you have experimented with the Doubting Chorus, teach students the difference between opinions and facts (see following pages). They are then ready for a mock competition. Call it an Essay Slam. See "Try This 12" on how to put together an Essay Slam.

Discussion

What is the difference between persuading someone in an essay and persuading your parents? Will methods that work in speech work on paper? What skills do you need to be truly persuasive on paper?

Try This 12: Essay Slam

Here's how to put together your own Essay Slam:

1. Place a podium in front of the class and have a student reader stand there.
2. Elect a panel of three judges. More judges may be used, but the total must be an odd number.
3. Give each judge an arrow. The arrow is used for pointing towards the winner.
4. The rest of the class becomes the doubting chorus. It is their job to doubt the reader any time he pauses.
5. Choose a student to come to the podium to read. Before they are allowed to read, they must go through their essay and underline all the facts.

6. Once the student reader is at the podium, he/she may only pound a fist on the podium for facts, not opinions. Ask students to underline facts before they come up to perform their piece.

7. The judges are in charge of deciding who has won the competition: the Doubting Chorus or the reader. Each judge will point his or her arrow at whomever he/she feels has won the competition.

I know kids should pick their own bedtimes. WHY? Because I am a kid. We know how much sleep we need. We know how much time it will take to get our homework done. Besides that it is not fair because your parents get to watch T.V. T.V is sometimes learning. And if you are not tired, you just lay in bed and do nothing when you could be reading. And if you have a younger sister or brother they should go to bed earlier than you should. I know kids should pick there own bedtimes. By the age of 8 we are old enough to make all our own decisions.

Try This 13: Separating Facts from Opinions

Choose any topic. Now list opinions about that topic and facts about that same topic. What is the difference? How can you tell the difference? This is a good lesson to do before an essay slam to help you prepare.

Topic:

My Opinions:

Facts:

Try This 14: Find the Sweet Spot Below a Position

Under every conflict lie the interests of both parties. Effective persuaders argue to the other parties' interests, not their own. The sweet spot is where both interests overlap (see the diagram on the next page). This activity helps your students weed out their weakest arguments from their best ones.

1) Talk to your students about conflict. Conflict happens when one person wants something, but another person wants something else. Pick a situation and ask for 2 volunteers.

2) One actor plays one position, the other actor plays the other position. Tell the students what their goal is—what they should be arguing for. This should be easy and familiar. Let's take an example:

   Child: I want a friend over.
   Mother: NO!

3) Now talk to your students about the interests of each person. Underneath the conflict lie these interests. See diagram next page. Tell students that their strongest points speak to their opponents interests, not their own. What are the interests of the other side? What is the underlying reason for each person's argument? Example: Mother wants it quiet. That's why she doesn't want her child to have a friend over.

4) Child's argument: We will play outside!

5) Final activity: Write a 2 page play where page one is all conflict and page two displays one side arguing to the other person's interests (the sweet spot).

6) Act out the plays and talk about the power of arguing to the other side.

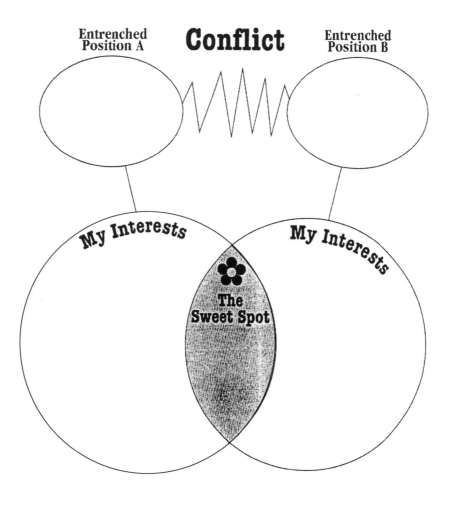

*From Why We Must Run with Scissors: Voice Lessons in Persuasive Writing,
by Barry Lane and Gretchen Bernabei. Used with Permission*

Those who only know their side of an argument know little of that.

—John Stuart Mill

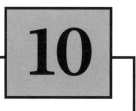

Insert Snapshots

The Point

A snapshot is a word picture that you add to your writing to pull the reader into the physical world. When students write with snapshots they bring the world into sharp focus for the reader. Strong writers use snapshots regularly and, on a writing test, just one snapshot in the right spot can be the difference between a passing score and the highest score.

What You Do

Bring a camera into class and talk to your students about what it means to take pictures with words. Snap a picture in the morning and print it in time for the writing lesson. Put it on an overhead and, as a class, draft a description of the photo.

Tell your students that, as a writer, they have a magic camera that can record smells, sounds, touch and taste as well as sight (see *senses* segment). This camera develops its film inside the reader's mind with the light of the reader's imagination. When we are bored with our writing, so is the reader. Snapshots are a way of drawing the reader into the writing.

Show the Inserting Snapshots segment to the class and try the activity on the video (see next page). Follow-up by asking students to look for places to add snapshots throughout their writing. Practice writing snapshots by looking at a photo and turning it into a word picture.

Discussion

How do snapshots improve a piece of writing? When should you cut snapshots?

Try This 15: Snapshot Leads

Pick one of the following prompts and write a snapshot lead. Does your writing paint a picture in the reader's head?

- Write about your favorite dessert.
- Write about your favorite season.
- Write about your favorite sport.

Here are examples of two leads to the same prompt. Which piece do you want to keep reading?

Example 1

Do you have a favorite dessert? Well, I do. My favorite desert is pumpkin pie. There are three reasons why I love pumpkin pie. The first reason is the smooth texture, the second reason is the rich color and the final reason is the spicy flavor that clings to the roof of your mouth.

Example 2

"Hey, Mom, what's for dessert?" I ask. I ask because sometimes I have a choice and sometimes I have several choices. Whenever I have a chance to eat pumpkin pie, I'll hog it.

Pumpkin pie has some kind of slickness that makes you want to lick it, the color of it makes you want to wear it, the texture of it makes you want to pick it up and throw it in somebody's face and then blame it on somebody else, and, of course, it makes you want to eat it.

Write a Snapshot Lead for the photo.

Write a Snapshot Lead for the photo.

_____

_____

_____

_____

_____

_____

_____

_____

_____

_____

_____

_____

_____

_____

_____

_____

_____

_____

Write a Snapshot Lead for the photo.

Try This 16: End with a Snapshot to be More Persuasive

In a persuasive essay, a snapshot can make the most compelling conclusion. The following example by high school student Becky Pinero, from our book *Why We Must Run with Scissors,* makes the point about saving the football program by painting a snapshot of the world without football in the reader's brain. Compare Becky's version below with the standard, "In conclusion, I feel we should not cancel the football program for three reasons . . ." and see the power of snapshots to capture the reader's attention and imagination.

> *So I hope you decide not to cancel the football program this year. But if you don't, just imagine. You're driving down the freeway on a Friday night in September. Your car approaches Alamo Stadium. You glance over your shoulder, out the window, and what to you see? The parking lot is dark and empty. The stadium lights are dark. The quiet is deafening. There are no school buses, no crowds of parents, no shouts of cheerleaders, no bands playing. As you drive past, you will wonder . . . where is everyone? Sir, don't let this happen.*
>
> Reprinted from *Why We Must Run with Scissors: Voice Lessons in Persuasive Writing* by Barry Lane and Gretchen Bernabei (overhead on next page)

Ending a piece of writing with a snapshot is not only more entertaining but more memorable, as well. Read the following ending to a story and write your own snapshot conclusion. How do they differ?

> *In closing, I think that Summer is better than Winter for these three reasons . . .*

The Snapshot Ending

So, I hope you decide not to cancel the football program this year. But if you don't, just imagine. You're driving down the freeway on a Friday night in September. Your car approaches Alamo Stadium. You glance over your shoulder, out the window, and what to you see? The parking lot is dark and empty. The stadium lights are dark. The quiet is deafening. There are no school buses, no crowds of parents, no shouts of cheerleaders, no bands playing. As you drive past, you will wonder . . . where is everyone? Sir, don't let this happen.

Reprinted from *Why We Must Run with Scissors: Voice Lessons in Persuasive Writing* by Barry Lane and Gretchen Bernabei

Explode the Moment

The Point

The best way to pull a reader in on a test response is to find focus in writing. Too many writers just move from one paragraph to the next without really developing a point. For a narrative prompt, the best way to find a focus is to choose one important moment and then explode that moment over the entire page. This moment might be only a few seconds or a few minutes, but it is a moment that the writer wants to make unforgettable. A student writer who enjoys exploding moments will be able to do so even when given a dud prompt. The craft of writing will pull the pen along. In this lesson, I'm generating excitement about writing in slow motion.

What You Do

Have students act out slow motion moments like I did on the video. Kids love doing this and you can ask them what they noticed in slow motion that they didn't see in fast motion. Good moments to try include reunion scenes, running scenes or great moments in sports.

Read slow motion moments from literature or test responses. Notice how a student writing in slow motion tends to develop a sharper, more meaningful focus in his/her writing.

Here's a lesson I love doing with kids. Ask them to pretend to be filmmakers creating documentaries of their lives. Where would they use slow motion? Have students fill a page with one short moment. When they get stuck, discourage them from writing big or adding extra words. Instead, have them try switching from snapshots (descriptive writing,) to thoughtshots (internal reflective writing) to, perhaps, a bit of dialogue.

Have students complete the "Explode a Moment" activity on the following page. Once students know how to explode moments, encourage them to look for slow motion opportunities in their writing.

Discussion

How can exploding a moment improve a piece of writing? When might it weaken a piece of writing? Is there a moment in your story you would like to explode?

Idea excerpted from *After THE END* and *Reviser's Toolbox* by Barry Lane.

Tips for Exploding a Moment

So, how do you explode a moment? Try using these tools to help you.

Snapshots: Physical pictures

Thoughtshots: What's going on in your head?

Dialogue: What are people saying?

Zooming in: Ask yourself questions to dig up small details to make a moment come alive.

Outside/Inside: Switch between Snapshots and Thoughtshots to make your moment last longer.

Try this 17: Explode a Moment

To practice, choose one of the following writing prompts. Instead of just answering the prompt, use it as an opportunity to explode a moment.

- There is a new box in the attic of your house. Pretend you are going to open it. Write about it.
- Write about a special person in your life.
- Write about an exciting time in your life.
- Write about your favorite sport.

Make your choice of what to write about by brainstorming a few lists first.

Example:

Exciting times: The moment I met my dog
Riding a bull at the farm
Getting caught by my brother

Tip: When exploding a moment about opening a box, do most of your exploding before the moment you open the box. Study the following example for some tricks you can use. Understand that the writer has no idea what is in the box or his mother's dark secret. It's okay to find these answers through the writing.

Example:

There is a box in your attic. Write about what you might find when you open it.

I crept up the creaking attic stairs, gripping the box cutter in my left hand and sliding up the handrail with my right. With each slow step I could feel the tension building, twisting inside my stomach like some caged animal. What would I find when I opened the mysterious box my dead aunt had left there? How could I know if the promise she made me was really true? What would Mother think when she realized that I knew the darkest secret about her childhood in New Jersey?

My knees buckled, and I could feel a cloud of sadness wash over me as my hand touched the bronze doorknob at the top of the stairs. Was I ready to step into that dark room? What would be left of my childhood once I knew the truth?

As the door creaked open, a blast of musty air slapped me in the face like an old memory that you just couldn't forget no matter how hard you tried. My eyes scanned the room. There was a pile of old busted chairs, a stack of moldy books with ripped out pages strewn like leaves across the floor, and, beyond it all in the far corner, sitting on a tray table, was the box that held my destiny.

When to Explode a Moment

- A moment of tension
- A moment of discovery
- A moment of confrontation
- A moment of transformation
- A moment of fear
- A moment of embarrassment
- A moment of despair
- A funny moment
- A moment of confusion
- A moment of triumph
- A moment of defeat
- A moment of betrayal
- A moment of discovery
- A moment of sadness

**Don't just answer the prompt,
EXPLODE IT!**

Spark Your Imagination

The Point

Imagination is the fuel from which all words grow. Yet most students and teachers are afraid to get imaginative on a writing test. Author Vicki Spandel says, "We put the bird in a cage, lock the door, then tell it to fly away." No wonder we don't get results. So how do we help students to free their minds, even on a writing test? First off, they have to know that the test is not a big Napoleonic trial where they are guilty until proven innocent. They have to feel that they are great the way they are and the test is a chance to celebrate and imagine that greatness. I included the segment at Fort Ticonderoga to whet their appetite for this celebrating. I encourage you to add your own spin to this crazy top.

What You Do

Encourage students to approach boring test prompts from a new direction. "Write about an exciting moment in your life" might seem like a boring prompt until you realize you could pretend you are a historical figure. Most test scorers would love to read a piece that began, "An exciting time in my life is when I met the great Julius Caesar. . ." THEY DON'T CARE IF IT'S TRUE OR NOT. The trouble with going this route is that most students could not support their writing with enough detail. That's why I encourage students to use the test as a chance to work in some of the facts and ideas they have studied in any subject. Their writing can really start to take shape with the addition of interesting details they may have learned in science or history class. Students need not be limited to things they have learned in writing class.

When given a prompt like, "Write about a new door in your bedroom that leads to a magical place," many more literal-minded students will think, " There is no new door in my bedroom. What are they talking about?" But, if students understand that this prompt is not referring to *their* bedroom at all and that they are allowed to use their imagination, it becomes okay to have some fun with their writing. Explain this to your students and post the following page in your class. Teach students to free their minds.

They don't care if it's true or not.

Make it up!

Try This 18: Fake Writing Day

One way to look at test day is to re-name it Fake Writing Day: The Day You Get to Become a Magician and Fake-out the Audience with Your Imagination. Here are some prompts that require great fake-out skill. Read the following writing prompts and create some of your own challenging prompts. Celebrate Fake Writing Day! Have students begin by listing three reasons and then writing their responses.

Write about why you love homework.

Write about why you love spinach and liver.

Why do you hate ice cream? Explain.

Why should we cancel recess until the end of the year?

List Three Reasons

_____
_____
_____
_____
_____
_____
_____
_____
_____
_____
_____
_____
_____

Use your Imagination to Wake up Sleeping Assignments

Your imagination is what turns a boring writing assignment into an exciting activity that you can sink your teeth into. But how do you know when to use your imagination? Here are some tips on how to think about writing prompts using your imagination. Share them with your students and practice the imaginative voice.

When they say . . .	Your imagination says . . .
Write about a new door in your room which leads to a magical place	*I don't have a door in my bedroom and I don't want one. I'll just invent a totally new bedroom with 15 doors-a dream bedroom! YES!*
Write about an exciting time in your life.	*My life is boring, but I could invent a more interesting life. Let's see. I could write about the time I hit the game-winning homerun. And my writing will be so convincing that they will never know that I was cut from the Little League team at the first tryout.*
Write whether you believe in school uniforms.	*I don't care about school uniforms, but if we were all dressed as Superman, I would like that. Perhaps I could build a case for school superhero uniforms. Yes!*

Cleopatra's Test

If your students are bored out of their minds and want a highly challenging way to respond to a writing test prompt, ask them to try becoming a figure out of history. On the next page is Cleopatra's writing test. This can be great fun and get you the highest score to boot. Recommended for only the most precocious middle school students. You really need to know your history to pull this off!

Write about an exciting moment in your life.

An exciting moment in my life was when I met the great Julius Caesar, and, with his magnificent help, became Queen of all Egypt. Caesar had just landed with an army of 10,000 to attack my brother Ptolemy XIII's forces. My handmaidens rolled me up in a Persian carpet and smuggled me through the Roman lines and into Caesar's tent. Within a few hours, he and I were good friends.

And two years later, I would bear him a son, Caesarion, on June 23, 43 B.C. (by the way—it was a natural childbirth.) My brother was not pleased and drowned in the Nile trying to escape. As we say in Macedonia, silt happens.

Another exciting time in my life was when I went to Rome in 46 B.C. Julius was given a ten-year dictatorship, and I was heralded as his Egyptian prize. I started calling myself the new Egyptian goddess Isis. It was really neat 'cause all these old Roman guys got all bent out of shape when Caesar made a statue of me out of gold and placed it beside his in the Temple of Venus Venetrix. He said he would marry me even though technically you're only supposed to have one wife in Rome. He was a very smart guy. Everything changed on the ides of March, that's the day Caesar was killed and didn't leave me or his son a penny in his will. Eventually Mark Anthony, that big gorilla of a guy, came and I married him. That took about two seconds of eyelash batting to accomplish. (He was also married already but, like Caesar, that didn't seem to bother him.)

But the most exciting time in my life was 34 B.C. when my son Caesarion and I were crowned queen and king of Egypt, co-ruling with Anthony. They called me the new Isis and Anthony the new Dionysus. Caesarion was the king of kings and I was the queen of kings. It was all a little confusing, but that's okay, because by 30 B.C. Octavian had crushed us with his army. Anthony had fallen on his sword and I was supposed to be paraded through the streets like some circus monkey. In your dreams. I got my faithful servants to smuggle a cobra into my chamber in a basket of figs.

Legend has it that when you are bitten by a cobra, you live forever. After living my exciting life, maybe that wasn't such a good idea after all. I could use a rest. I hope you have enjoyed my story and will give me a high score.

Cleopatra, the New Isis

Reprinted from *51 Wacky We-Search Reports* by Barry Lane

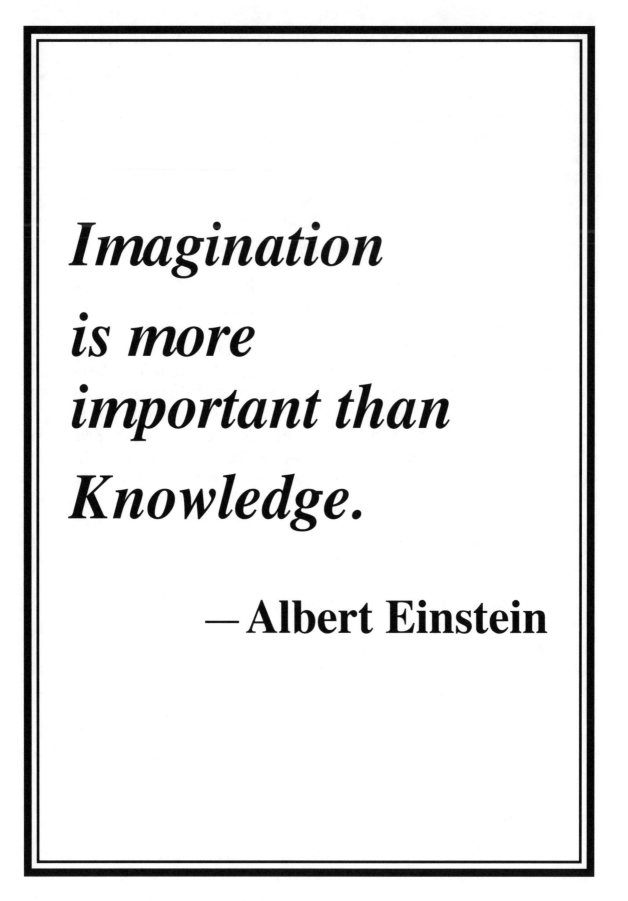

Imagination is more important than Knowledge.

— **Albert Einstein**

Give me Liberty and give me a high score, yeah!

When Ethan Allen and the Green Mountain Boys took Fort Ticonderoga on May 10th, 1775, they stormed the fort early in the morning when most of the British soldiers were still fast asleep. It seems an apt metaphor for the state writing test. The scorers are fast asleep and your students can awaken them from their slumber and capture their imaginations. I hope this DVD/VHS and what you do with it can supply ammunition to give your students enough confidence and cunning to get the job done.

We would love to hear your success stories. Please encourage your students to submit their test essays to the Student Center at **www.discoverwriting.com.**

Fax us at
802-897-2084

or

write us at
Submissions
Discover Writing Press
PO 264
Shoreham, VT 05770

Historical Correction

On the video, I say that Ethan Allen and I got the cannons to bring to Boston to start the revolutionary war. I did not mean that Ethan Allen brought the cannons to Boston. That was, of course, the great unsung patriot, Henry Knox. You can read about this amazing journey in the book *1776* by David McCullough.

Also, we all know the Revolutionary War started at Lexington with the shot heard 'round the world and then at the Battle of Bunker Hill. Instead of saying that the cannons from Fort Ti started the Revolutionary War, I should have said that the cannons helped drive the British out of Boston.

Lastly, my Ghana tiger shirt was not the traditional garb of a colonial soldier.

Works Cited

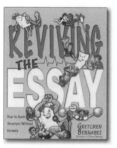

Reviving the Essay: How to Teach Structure Without Formula
by Gretchen Bernabei
This book contains dozens of voice building lessons that foster structured prose without force-feeding formulas.

Lightning in a Bottle (CD-ROM)
by Gretchen Bernabei
These 266 full-color photos and thematic insights can be

used to teach students how to mine insights from life and literature.

Reviser's ToolBox by Barry Lane
This practical sourcebook contains many pages that can be used to model lessons on revision for students.

After THE END by Barry Lane
Concepts like snapshots and thoughtshots, exploding moments and building scenes are explained and modeled in this popular professional book.

51 Wacky We-search Reports by Barry Lane
This book teaches multi-genre research with a funny twist. Richly illustrated and full of examples, this book helps students to find their voices when writing about subjects outside of themselves.

The Tortoise and the Hare Continued
by Barry Lane illustrated by Miles Bodimeade
Slow and steady wins the race. Not! This whimsical extension of Aesop fables teaches students to mine insights from stories.

Learning on Their Feet by Carol Glynn
Carol Glynn's comprehensive sourcebook teaches kinesthetic learning in 4 subjects, Science, Social Studies, Math and Language Arts.

Carol Out of the Box: Video Lessons in Kinesthetic Learning
by Carol Glynn.
(Includes copy of *Learning on Their Feet* with Video Guide or DVD)
These four 30-minute tapes contain entertaining lessons in kinesthetic learning that you can show directly to your class.

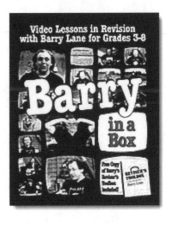

Barry In a Box: Student Lessons in Revision by Barry Lane
These 4 videos and 300-page *Reviser's Toolbox* guide are a complete set of mini-lessons for your classroom. Show the short lessons to your class and learn along with them.

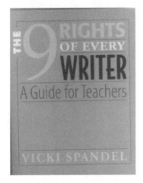

Quote from ***The 9 Rights of Every Writer***
by Vicki Spandel
In these days of hyper-assessment, it is sometimes easy to forget that the most important qualities of writing cannot be assessed. This inspirational book by Vicki Spandel shows us the rights we must protect for our students.

The School Essay Manifesto
by Thomas Newkirk
This short book will inspire you to change the way you think about teaching the school essay.

Why We Must Run with Scissors: Voice Lessons in Persuasive Writing
by Barry Lane and Gretchen Bernabei
82 two-page mini lessons that bring out voice in persuasive writing.

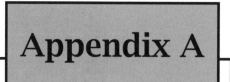

Gallery of
Test Scorers

(See DVD for Gallery of Test Scorers.)

Drawing by Robert Medrano

Drawing by Stanley Hayward

Drawing by Lauren Smith

Are you feeling sick? If you're feeling sick, I can get a waste paper basket and place it near your desk.

Photo of Linda Peake

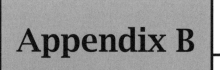

Photos to
Inspire Writing

Wisdom comes with age.

You can hide from your past but not your present.

Those who don't jump don't learn.

Liberty can't be built, only grown.

Wars start with walls.

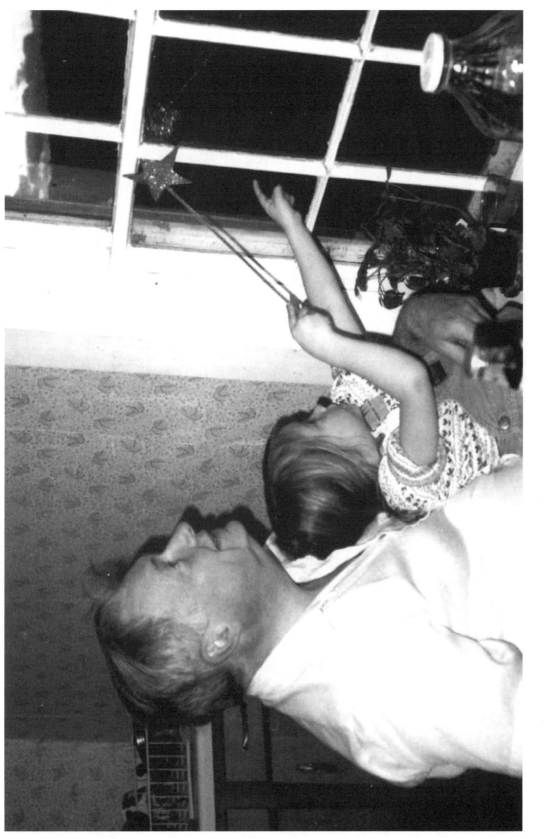

Wishes come before dreams come true.

Memory speaks. Fear listens.

Everyone needs somebody to look up to.

105

Teacher Professional Development: Lessons-To-Go

Besides using this video with students in the classroom, the same lessons can be used to train teachers in effective approaches to teaching writing and preparing students for a writing test. The teacher's understanding of these lessons will be greatly enhanced by the supplementary materials suggested in the following Professional Development day outlines. For a more in-depth study of ideas modeled in the *Hooked on Meaning* DVD, see the following pages for reading assignments, which parallel the video chapters. More Professional Development outlines are available by visiting the Teacher Center at **www.discoverwriting.com.**

Module 1—Messing with Text Structure

Understanding Sentence Structure; Create Unique Sentences (Chapter 3)

Teacher Discussion: How do you teach sentence structure? Do you teach students to write in sentences at all times or do you teach them to recognize sentences they have written? When and how do you teach students to write compound and compound complex sentences. (20 minutes: Small and Large group discussion)

Suggested Reading: *Reviving the Essay*, pages 128–131; Ba Da Bing Sentences (background pages 11 and 12; A Field Guide to Sentences, page 14); *Image Grammar* by Harry Noden; *Mechanically Inclined* by Jeff Anderson

Video Clip: Show chapter 2; Barry plays Larry Bane, the grammatically-challenged bank robber. This clip uses humor to open a discussion about the need to write in complete sentences.

Try this: (Chapter 3) Ba Da Bing

Teacher Discussion: After doing the activity, read your ba-da-bing sentence. What kind of sentence is it? How can ba-da-bing sentences help students to expand their range of understanding what a sentence is? How can this help pace their writing? What other lessons do you use to help students understand the wide variety of sentence structures?

Varying sentence structure: 30 minutes

Take a piece of mundane student writing and improve it with your group. Share your findings with the larger group. See *Reviving the Essay,* page 128.

Teacher Discussion: Did the writing get better when you re-wrote it? Will it typically get better? How do we help students write sentences of varying lengths? When is it appropriate to talk about sentences in a writing workshop?

Suggested Reading: *Mechanically Inclined* by Jeff Anderson (a wonderful handbook that teaches grammar in the context of student writing.)

Try this: Creating Text Structure, Grades 4–12: 2–5 hour workshop

The days of the 5 paragraph theme are long gone, yet the shadow still lingers in many class-rooms and school districts. To free the minds of your students, give them many text structures and encourage them to experiment. This workshop provides teachers with ideas and lessons for freeing students from formulaic writing.

Teacher Discussion: Why do students write boring responses on prompted writing tests? Does formula writing improve test scores? Is boring writing what scorers are looking for? If not, how can we wean students from formula writing and inspire them to write with passion and voice?

Suggested Reading: *The School Essay Manifesto* by Thomas Newkirk, Pages 1–80; *Reviving the Essay,* by Gretchen Bernabei, Lessons 1, 2, 3; *Lightning in a Bottle (CD-ROM)* by Gretchen Bernabei *Why We Must Run with Scissors* (lesson 23); *51 Wacky We-search Reports* (skim Multi-Genre lessons and pick one that would work as an alternative essay).

Video Clip: Build Bridges to the Reader's Mind

Try Truisms: 30 minutes

Follow the steps in the video lesson and in the lesson guide on Chapter 7, or use images and insights from Gretchen Bernabei's *Lightning in a Bottle* CD to develop your own lesson.

Once you have found your own truism, free-write for 30 minutes about that truth. Share your writings in small groups.

Opening Discussion: How do truisms help students on prompted tests? What are the drawbacks of teaching prompted writing this way? What are the payoffs? What other ways can we help students become individual thinkers?

Suggested Reading: *Reviving the Essay* by Gretchen Bernabei, Chapter 1.

The Multi-Genre Research Essay: 90 minutes

In many tests it is possible to play with a writing prompt. In fact, state standards promote the idea of multi-genre writing. Does this mean my essay on what ants eat can be written as a menu for the Ant Cafe? Yes, as long as I can include all the specific facts and information. "Try our Leaf Matter Platter. Sample milk from our all you can drink 'Aphid bar.'"

Suggested Reading: *51 Wacky We-search Reports*, pages 1–180 (Choose reports to experiment with by skimming the book).

Teacher Discussion: How does wacky we-search change the way students view non-fiction writing assignments? What scaffolding activities or pre-writing activities could you do to improve the outcome of a wacky we-search report? How could you design a rubric to assess a wacky we-search report?

Hamburger Helper: 90 minutes

Once students are confident with their interpretations, they can begin playing with the traditional structure of a test response.

Video Clip: View "Create New Text Structures." Discuss the hamburger paragraph and how paragraphs can come in more than one shape. See page 19, Hamburger Helper.

Suggested Reading: *The School Essay Manifesto* by Thomas Newkirk, Chapters 1–3; Read pages 19–88 in *Reviving the Essay* or make copies of pages 28–32 in this sourcebook.

Pick one or two structures to experiment with.

Teacher Discussion: How do these structures work with students? Will this lesson work with all students? How does a traditional text structure help students? How can we teach structure without formula? Is it possible to use different structures when taking the state writing test? How does structure affect content? How does content affect structure in writing? Which of the structures we explored be most effective with the students you teach?

Pacing a Narrative — Snapshots and Thoughtshots and Exploding Moments: 90 to 160 minute workshop

Interesting writing has a texture and a pace. The events and ideas are not all evenly weighted; some are more important than others. This is usually reflected in the amount of text a writer spends describing them. Time to a writer is like playdough in the hands of a toddler. This lesson has helped many teachers and students improve a piece through emphasis.

Suggested Reading: *After The End*, pages 31–79; *Reviser's Toolbox*, pages 74–95a; Video: *Barry In a Box*, Tape 3.

Video Clip: *Barry in a Box*, Tape 3, Snapshots and Thoughtshots: View chapter, "Insert Snapshot."

Teacher Discussion: How do we help students to enhance their thoughts so as to expand their writing? How can snapshots and thoughtshots improve a test response? What are the drawbacks of teaching concepts like snapshots and thoughtshots?

Explode a Moment: 2–4 hour workshop

One of the best lessons I have ever presented teaches students to expand an important moment in a narrative.

Suggested Reading: *After the End*, Chapter 5; *Reviser's Toolbox*, Chapter 4; *Hooked on Meaning*, Chapter 11; *Barry in a Box*, Tape 4.

Video Clip: View Chapter 11 in *Hooked on Meaning* and discuss the strategy of writing in slow motion. For a more in-depth lesson, view Tape 4 from *Barry in a Box* and do the activities.

Read examples of "exploded moments" from literature. These are moments where the author slows down time for dramatic effect.

Teacher Discussion: Will exploding a moment help a student score well on your state writing test? How do you turn a writing prompt into an exploded moment? What narrative techniques do students need to know in order to explode a moment?

Try This: Make Text-to-Text and Text-to-Life Connections: 30 Minutes

Many writing tests reward students who know how to make text-to-text and text-to-life connections. The ability to make these connections also gives students creative ideas to enhance their writing in ways that will wake up their readers.

Suggested Reading: *Why We Must Run with Scissors: Voice Lessons in Persuasive Writing,* Lesson 23

Here is a mini-lesson that teaches students to make these connections and grow insights into their writing prompts.

1. Ask students to look at a photograph and truism. See Appendix B.
2. Have them write for five minutes about what the photo means to them.

3. Ask them to stop and read over what they have written.
4. Now have them write for ten more minutes about a movie or book this photo reminds them of. Stop.
5. Now have them read over what they have written and write again, this time about an experience in their life

Teacher Discussion: How did your essay change each time you wrote? Could you find connections with literature? Or movies or life? How could this activity be used to prepare students for a writing test?

For more professional development lessons visit the Teacher Center at
www.discoverwriting.com

Appendix D

Quotes to
Inspire Writers

Writers write for the same reason readers read—to find out what's going to happen.

—Elmore Leonard

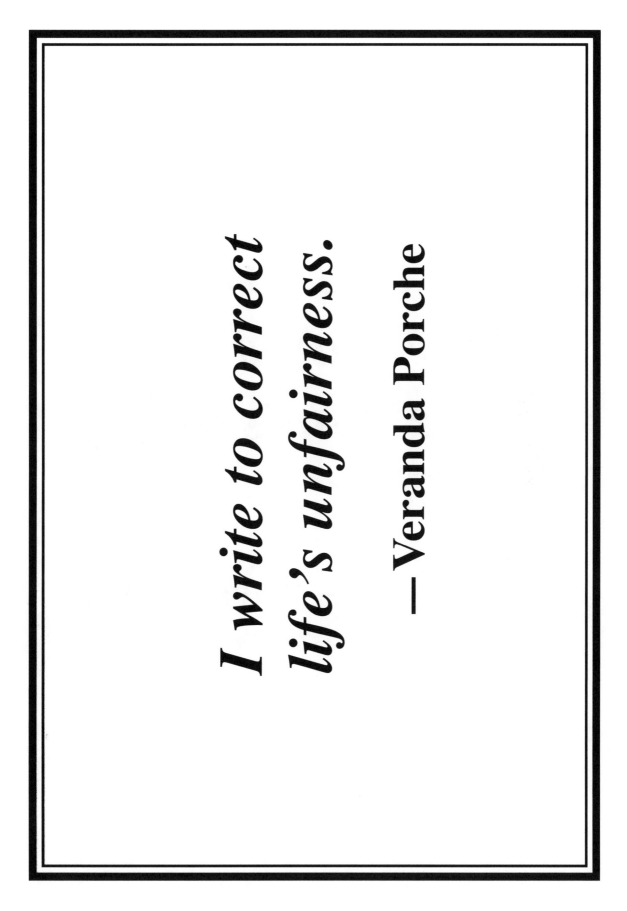

I write to correct life's unfairness.

—Veranda Porche

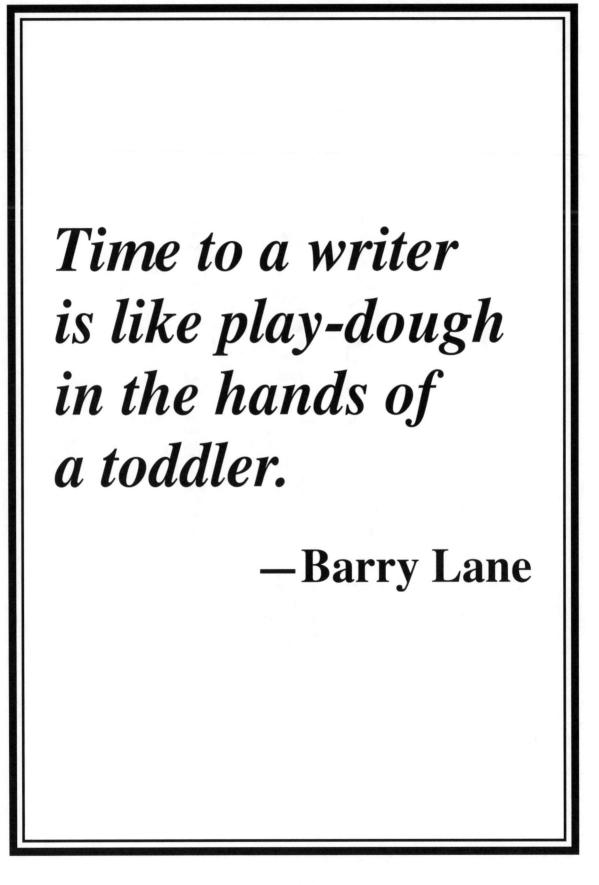

Time to a writer is like play-dough in the hands of a toddler.

—Barry Lane

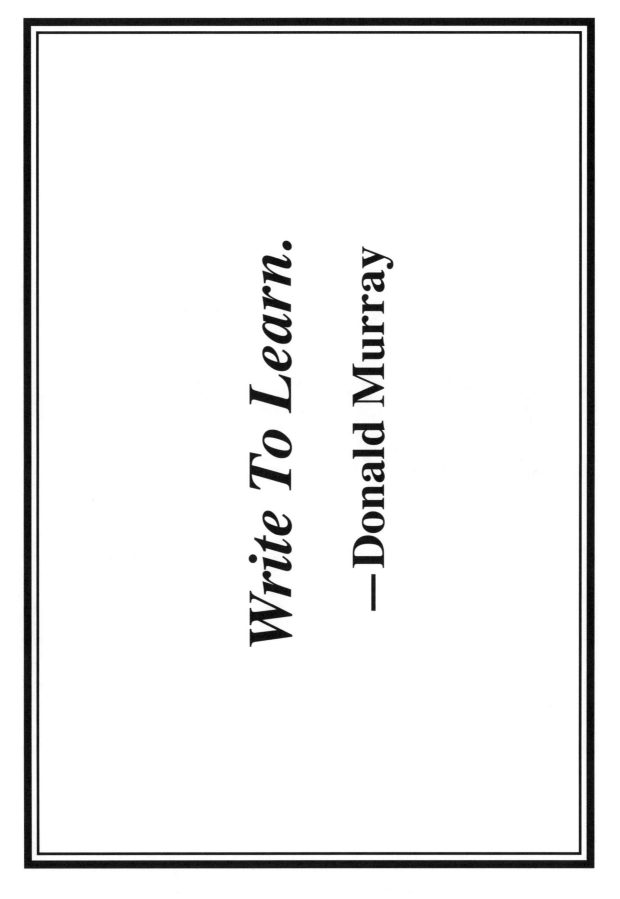

Write To Learn.

—Donald Murray

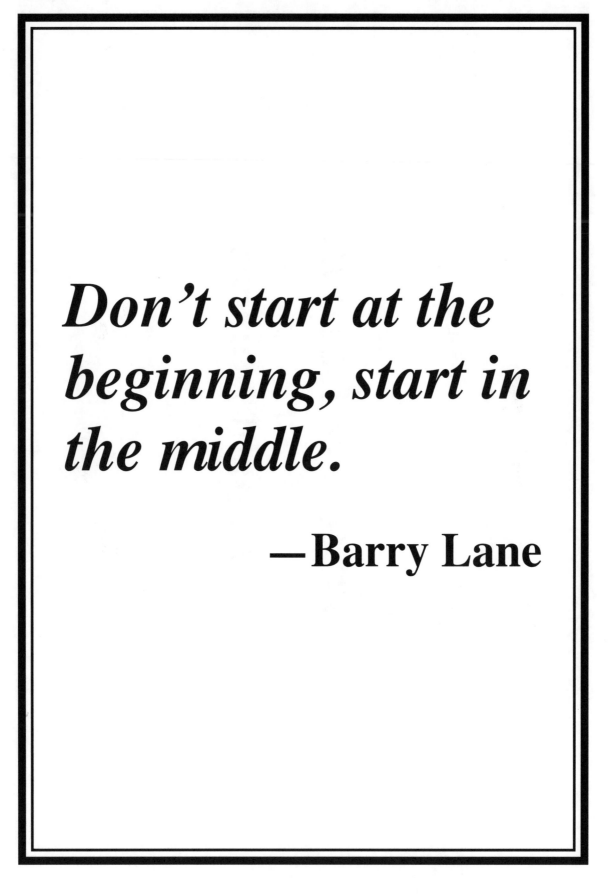

Don't start at the beginning, start in the middle.

—**Barry Lane**

Make your awkwardness work for you. If you can't describe the beauty of the tree, write about how you can't describe it and soon you will be describing it.

—**Geof Hewitt**

Discover Writing Press

Visit the Discover Writing website at

www.discoverwriting.com

to find more lessons, submit student work, order Discover Writing books and videos or book Barry Lane and other authors for a visit to your school district.